Canada

John Sylvester

MACDONALD YOUNG BOOKS

First published in 1995 by Macdonald Young Books Ltd
© Macdonald Young Books Ltd 1995

Macdonald Young Books Ltd
Campus 400
Maylands Avenue
Hemel Hempstead
Herts HP2 7EZ

Design Roger Kohn
Editor Diana Russell
DTP editor Helen Swansbourne
Picture research John Sylvester, Valerie Mulcahy
Illustration János Márffy
Commissioning editor Debbie Fox

Special thanks to Nicky Cleaveland of the
Prince Edward Island Government Services Library

We are grateful to the following for permission
to reproduce photographs:
Front cover: John Sylvester *above* and *below*;
Bryan and Cherry Alexander, pages 17, 23, 26; First Light,
Toronto, pages 8/9 *above* (Ken Straiton), 11 *above* (Richard Hartmier),
12 (Brian Milne), 13 *below* (Robert Semenuik), 14
(Jerry Kobalenko), 16 *above* (Grant Black) and *below*
(David Nunuk), 18 (Larry Macdougal), 19, 22 (Jessie Parker), 24
below (Dave Reede), 24/25 (Pat Morrow), 25 *below*, 28 *above*
(Tom Kitchin), 31 (Ken Straiton), 32/33, 34 (Tom Kitchin),
35 *below*, 37 (Pat Morrow), 38 (Richard Hartmier), 39 *above*
(Chris Harris), 40 *above*, 43 (Tom Kitchin); Robert Harding
Picture Library, page 35 *above*; Roger Kohn, page 21 *below*;
Reflexion, pages 21 *above* (Ives Tessier), 29 (Sheila Naimen),
30 (Michel Gascon); Tony Stone Images, pages 28 *below*
(Kevin Miller), 41 (David E Myers); John Sylvester, pages 8, 11
below, 13 *above*, 15, 20, 24 *above left*, 27, 32 *below*, 33 *below*,
39 *below*, 40 *below*, 42; Telegraph Colour Library
(Colorific), page 36 (George Zimbel)

The statistics given in this book are the most up to date
available at the time of going to press

Printed and bound in Portugal by Edições ASA

⊃ catalogue record for this book is available from
the British Library

ISBN: 0 7500 1771 6

PROVINCE	AREA (sq km)	CAPITAL	POPULATION (1992 estimate)	DATE JOINED CANADIAN CONFEDERATION
Newfoundland	405,720	St John's	581,100	1949
Nova Scotia	55,490	Halifax	920,800	1867
New Brunswick	73,440	Fredericton	749,100	1867
Prince Edward Island	5,660	Charlottetown	130,300	1873
Quebec	1,540,660	Quebec City	7,150,700	1867
Ontario	1,068,580	Toronto	10,609,800	1867
Manitoba	649,940	Winnipeg	1,113,100	1870
Saskatchewan	652,330	Regina	1,004,500	1905
Alberta	661,190	Edmonton	2,632,400	1905
	947,800	Victoria	3,451,300	1871
				ESTABLISHED
	483,450	Whitehorse	30,200	1898
	3,426,320	Yellowknife	62,300	1870

ARCTIC OCEAN

105°

Cape Columbia

ELLESMERE ISLAND

GREENLAND

Iqaluit

LABRADOR SEA

NEWFOUNDLAND

Twillingate

Gander

St John's

QUEBEC

A

PRINCE EDWARD ISLAND

Cavendish

Charlottetown

NEW BRUNSWICK

Quebec

Fredericton

Halifax

NOVA SCOTIA

ATLANTIC OCEAN

ONTARIO

Saskatoon

SASKATCHEWAN

Regina

Winnipeg

Thunder Bay

Montreal

Hull

OTTAWA

Pickering

Toronto

Hamilton

Fort Erie

USA

0   1,000 km

CONTENTS

Words that are explained in the glossary are printed in
SMALL CAPITALS the first time they are mentioned in the text.

▌◀ INTRODUCTION

Canada is the second largest country in the world (after the Russian Federation). Its relatively small population of 28.7 million people live in only 11% of the country's area.

Canadians have exploited their country's wealth of natural resources to build one of the world's richest societies. The highly industrialized economy produces items ranging from paper and steel to communications satellites and nuclear reactors. Canada is the world's seventh largest economy, after the USA, Japan, Germany, France, Italy and the UK.

As well as a high standard of material wealth, Canadians enjoy cleaner air, lower crime rates, and better health and education than many industrialized countries. These

▲ *Toronto is Canada's largest city. Its distinctive skyline is dominated by the CN tower, the world's largest free-standing structure.*

◀ *Moraine Lake is just one of many lakes in the Rocky Mountains created by melting* GLACIERS. *This famous view was once pictured on the Can $10 note.*

are some reasons why in 1994 the United Nations rated Canada the best country in the world to live in.

Canada was once a British colony. It is still a member of the Commonwealth. However, since the end of the Second World War, ties to Britain have steadily declined. The most important influence today is the USA. With a population ten times larger than Canada's, its influence can be overwhelming. The two countries share the longest undefended border in the world – 8,890 kilometres. Most Canadians live less than a day's drive from the border. But they don't have to cross it to experience American culture. They just turn on their televisions. Some 64% of the programmes they watch are from the USA.

In the province of Quebec, 82% of people speak French as their first language. Their society and culture are unique, and very different from English Canada's. Many Quebecers would like to protect their culture by separating from Canada to form their own country. Finding a way for people of French and English origin to live together in harmony has always been Canada's greatest challenge.

■ THE LANDSCAPE

Canada stretches 5,500 kilometres from east to west — one-quarter of the distance around the world. Its most southerly point, Middle Island in Lake Erie, shares the same latitude as the French Riviera, while the most northerly point, Cape Columbia on Ellesmere Island, is only 768 km from the North Pole. In between lies 4,000 km of mostly wilderness.

There are six geographical regions. The Canadian Shield is the largest, occupying nearly half of the country's area. It takes its name from the hard bedrock that underlies the region. It is noted for its many lakes and rivers, thin soil, dense forests and abundant wildlife. Most of Lake Superior — the largest fresh water lake in the world — lies within the region.

Boreal forest covers much of the Canadian Shield. This is a mixture of evergreen trees such as pine, spruce, fir and cedar, and a few deciduous trees such as birch and aspen. The forest is home to beavers, moose, black bears, wolves, lynx, porcupines and many other animals.

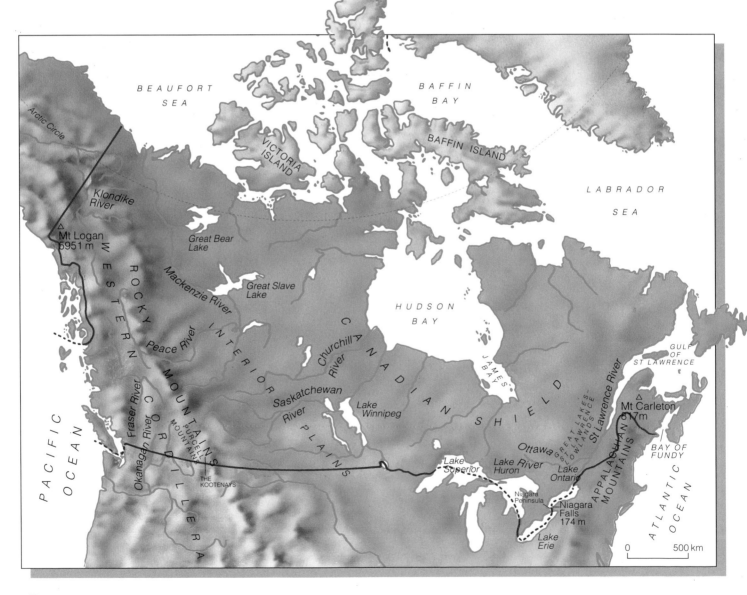

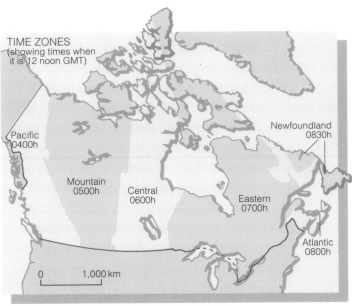

TIME ZONES
(showing times when
it is 12 noon GMT)

Pacific
0400h

Mountain
0500h

Central
0600h

Eastern
0700h

Atlantic
0800h

Newfoundland
0830h

0   1,000 km

▲ Lake Superior is the largest of the Great Lakes. Its rocky northern shore is part of the Canadian Shield.

▼ The spectacular Rocky Mountains were formed by movements in the Earth's surface some 60 million years ago.

Canada is the coldest country in the world. Its average annual temperature is only –5.6°C.

In the Arctic, the ground is permanently frozen. This PERMAFROST underlies more than 40% of the country. But the Arctic receives less snowfall than the rest of Canada. If it were not for the cold temperatures, the area would be a desert. Canada's coldest weather station is at Eureka, Ellesmere Island, with an average annual temperature of –19.7°C.

The warm Pacific Ocean means the west coast has the mildest winters. This area also has the most rain. Prince Rupert, 500 km north of Vancouver, receives 2,400 mm of precipitation (rain and snow) a year.

The Cordillera Mountains stop the moist Pacific air from moving further east. Winters

▲ *Every winter, snowstorms bring traffic to a stop in Canadian cities. Here, people in Toronto dig their cars out of the snow.*

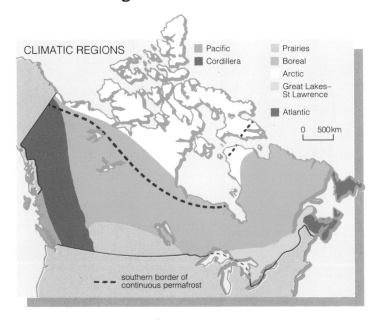

CLIMATIC REGIONS

Pacific
Cordillera
Prairies
Boreal
Arctic
Great Lakes–St Lawrence
Atlantic

0   500km

- - - southern border of continuous permafrost

here are cold and summers are cool. The western slopes receive as much as 600 cm of snow annually. This allows residents of Vancouver to play golf in the morning, then drive 100 km to the mountains for an afternoon of skiing.

Most of the southern prairies, on the other side of the mountains, have less than 400 mm of precipitation a year. Far from the moderating effects of the ocean, the prairies have an extreme (continental) climate, with cold winters and hot, dry summers. Lack of rain, combined with high temperatures and wind, can produce severe drought.

The vast Boreal (forest) region and the Great Lakes–St Lawrence lowlands also have a continental climate, but with more precipitation. Montreal has about 235 cm of snow annually, more than any other major city in the world.

Atlantic Canada has some of the worst weather. Violent winter storms blow from the Atlantic Ocean, bringing heavy snow and freezing rain. St John's, Newfoundland, is the snowiest, foggiest, wettest, windiest and cloudiest city in Canada. It also has the most freezing rain.

KEY FACTS

● About 30% of Canada's annual precipitation falls as snow.
● The country's coldest recorded temperature was –63°C in Snag, Yukon, on 3 February 1947.
● In January 1962 in Pincher Creek, Alberta, a warm, dry wind known as a CHINOOK raised the temperature from –19°C to 22°C in just 1 hour.
● Canada's most intense heatwave struck the prairie provinces in July 1936, lasting 1½ weeks. Temperatures reached 44.4°C and 780 people died.

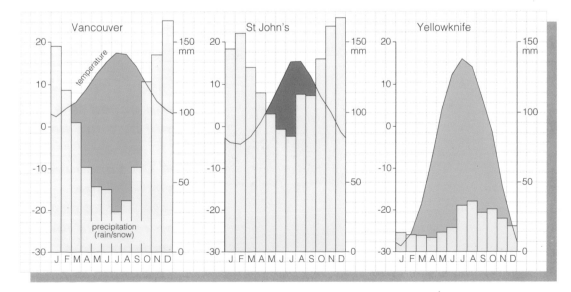

▲ *Canadians take maximum advantage of their short summers by flocking to beaches such as this one in Cavendish, Prince Edward Island.*

more than 8 million immigrants.

During the early 1900s the government attracted settlers to western Canada by offering them cheap farmland. When there was mass unemployment across the world in the 1930s, more people left Canada than entered. However, immigration picked up again after the Second World War when Canada's expanding economy needed skilled workers.

Until the 1960s, the majority of immigrants came from Britain and Europe. Today, most come from Asia. Some are refugees fleeing political oppression and war in their own countries. Others are seeking new business opportunities. Most settle in cities. Vancouver, for example, is home to many people from Hong Kong who left the British colony to avoid living under Chinese rule (Hong Kong will become part of China in 1997).

KEY FACTS

● The population in 1867 (3.4 million) was less than that of Toronto today.
● The Northwest Territories cover more than a third of Canada's area but contain less than 1% of its population.
● 80% of Canadians live within 320 km of the US border.
● 53 Native languages are still spoken in Canada. The most widely known are Cree, Ojibwa and Inuktitut.

CITIES

In 1851, when Canada was still a British colony, only 13% of people lived in cities. The proportion of city-dwellers has increased steadily since then. Now three-quarters of Canadians live in cities. Ontario is the most urbanized province – about 83% of the population live in a town or city. British Columbia and Alberta are next, with about 79%. Prince Edward Island is the least urbanized province, with two-thirds of its residents living in rural areas.

◀ *These children are taking part in a* POW-WOW *at the Six Nations Reserve in Ontario. The festival of traditional music and dance is a popular way for Native people to celebrate their culture.*

DAILY LIFE

▲ *When Ottawa's Rideau Canal freezes over in winter, it becomes the world's longest skating rink and a popular spot for the city's residents.*

Canadians enjoy a very high standard of living. The average family income in 1991 was about Can $53,000, compared with Can $41,000 in the USA. Six out of ten families live in detached homes, usually in the suburbs. Families are small – 1.8 children per couple – and in 60% of households, both parents work.

EDUCATION

Some 89% of Canadians between the ages of six and 23 attend school, college or university: the highest attendance rate in the world. In the USA the figure is 86%; in Britain it is 72%. The world average is 49%.

School is compulsory until the age of 16. It begins with kindergarten, followed by elementary school, junior high and high school. Most children attend publicly funded schools, but there are private schools too. After high school, at the age of 18, students with sufficiently high marks may attend one of Canada's 69 universities or 203 colleges.

The school year begins in September and ends in June. There are short breaks at Christmas and in March, with summer holidays in July and August. In some

▼ *The snow-mobile was invented by a Canadian in 1937. Snow-mobiling is now one of the fastest-growing winter pastimes in the country.*

farming regions, such as northern New Brunswick, students have a week off in the autumn to help with the harvest.

French immersion programmes provide instruction in French to those who do not use it as a first language. Since they were introduced in 1970, enrolment has grown steadily. More than 240,000 students are now involved.

LEISURE

Canada's long winters mean sports such as skiing, skating and ice-hockey are popular. Ice-hockey, invented in Montreal in 1885, is often called "Canada's game". Most of the players in the National Hockey League are Canadian, even though most teams are located in the USA. Baseball and American football are also popular team sports.

Canadians make the best of their short

▼ *Canadian children often learn to play ice-hockey on outdoor rinks like this one. Many dream of one day playing in the National Hockey League.*

KEY FACTS

● There are 64 televisions for every 100 people in Canada (compared with 81 in the USA and 43 in the UK), and 78 telephones per 100 people (79 in the USA and 46 in the UK).

● In 1992, the Toronto Blue Jays baseball team won the World Series – the first team outside the USA ever to do so. They won the series again in 1993.

● Lacrosse is the oldest organized sport in North America. It was originally a Native game called "baggatway".

● Alcoholism among the Native population is 13 times that of white Canadians, and their life expectancy is 10 years less than the Canadian average of 77 years.

▼ *Swimmers enjoy the wave pool at the world's largest indoor mall in Edmonton, Alberta.*

3

▲ **Heli-skiing in the Purcell Mountains of British Columbia. Skiers hire helicopters to take them to remote peaks for a downhill run through deep snow.**

RELIGIOUS DAYS AND HOLIDAYS

January 1	NEW YEAR'S DAY
March or April	EASTER
3rd Monday in May	VICTORIA DAY (Queen Victoria's birthday)
June 24	SAINT-JEAN BAPTISTE DAY (Quebec only)
July 1	CANADA DAY
1st Monday in August	CIVIC DAY (in most provinces)
1st Monday in September	LABOUR DAY
2nd Monday in October	THANKSGIVING DAY
November 11	REMEMBRANCE DAY
December 25	CHRISTMAS DAY
December 26	BOXING DAY

TRADE AND INDUSTRY

TRADE

More than 25% of Canada's goods and services are sold abroad, chiefly to the USA, which takes 75% of exports and provides 75% of imports. A free-trade agreement allows goods to pass duty-free (without taxes or tariffs) across the border. In 1993, the two countries signed the North America Free Trade Agreement with Mexico, creating the world's largest free-trade zone. It comes into full effect by 2003.

Canada's second largest trading partner is Japan, followed by the United Kingdom, Germany, France and South Korea.

Natural resources such as wheat, minerals and forestry products earned most of Canada's export income until very recently. More than 50% now comes from manufactured goods and services.

MANUFACTURING

Three-quarters of manufacturers are in central Canada. Ontario has more than 50%. Motor vehicles are the most important product. The 1965 Canada–United States Auto Pact agreement permits duty-free movement of vehicles and parts across the border. It also states that for every vehicle sold in Canada, one must be made there. This has helped Canada become the world's third largest exporter of motor vehicles, after Japan and Germany. Ontario also manufactures transport equipment (railway carriages), chemicals, electronic products, fabricated metals (including steel) and food products.

Quebec accounts for about 25% of Canada's manufacturing industries. Paper, food processing and textiles are the most important. The only other provinces with significant manufacturing are Alberta and British Columbia, with about 15%.

SERVICE INDUSTRIES

About 80% of all Canadian jobs are in service industries such as tourism, banking,

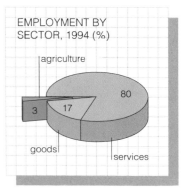

◄ *This mill on Vancouver Island produces pulp, which is used to make paper. Pulp exports are worth more than Can $4 billion a year.*

EMPLOYMENT BY SECTOR, 1994 (%)

agriculture
3
17
80
goods
services

KEY FACTS

● Canada launched the world's first domestic communications satellite, the Anik A-1, in 1972.

● Canada has 177 scientists and technicians per 1,000 people – 8 times the world average. Sweden is the world leader, with 262, while the USA has only 55.

● The Canadian work force totalled 13.8 million people in 1992. Women make up 45% of the total.

● The Candu nuclear generating station in Pickering, Ontario, is the largest producer of commercial nuclear power in the world.

● In 1939 a Czech immigrant, Thomas J Bata, founded Bata Shoes. It is now the largest shoe-making company in the world, selling 300 million pairs in 115 countries each year.

▲ *Vancouver is Canada's busiest port. Here railway containers carrying grain and other freight wait to be loaded on to ships.*

▶ *Motor-vehicle production is Canada's chief manufacturing industry. These vehicles are made by General Motors, the largest manufacturer.*

RUSSIA

Arctic Circle

BERING STRAIT

60°

BEAUFORT
SEA

USA

Holman
Island

YUKON

NORTHWEST

● Whitehorse

Yellowknife ●

PACIFIC

OCEAN

C

Prince Rupert ●

BRITISH
COLUMBIA

Edmonton ●

ALBERTA

Banff ●   Calgary ●

VANCOUVER
ISLAND

● Vancouver

Lethbridge ●

Pincher Creek ●   ●

Victoria ●

75°

60°

45°

30°

15°

0°

15°

30°

45°

90° 105° 120° 135° 150° 165° 180° 165° 150° 135° 120° 105° 90° 75° 60° 45° 30° 15° 0° 15° 30° 45° 60° 75° 90°